World Crafts and Recipes

Recipe and Craft Guide to

INDONESIA

Kayleen Reusser

Mitchell Lane

P.O. Box 196
Hockessin, Delaware 19707
Visit us on the web: www.mitchelllane.com
Comments? email us: mitchelllane@mitchelllane.com

Mitchell Lane

World Crafts and Recipes

The Caribbean • China • France
India • **Indonesia** • Japan

Library of Congress Cataloging-in-Publication Data
Reusser, Kayleen.
 Recipe and craft guide to Indonesia / by Kayleen Reusser.
  p. cm. — (World crafts and recipes)
 Includes bibliographical references and index.
 ISBN 978-1-58415-934-6 (library bound)
 1. Cookery, Indonesian—Juvenile literature. 2. Cookery—Indonesia.—Juvenile literature. I. Title.
 TX724.5.I5R49 2010
 641.59598—dc22

                                            2010009243

Printing   1   2   3   4   5   6   7   8   9

PLB

CONTENTS

I became interested in Indonesia when my daughter, Amanda, moved there in 2008 to teach high school English for two years. She began keeping a weblog ("blog") about her experiences. As I learned more about the country from her thoughts and photos, I became intrigued about this country on the other side of the world. I've included some of her photographs of Indonesia to help you get an insider's view of what it's like to live there.

In this book you'll find crafts and recipes of food dishes that reflect the heart of this country in Southeast Asia. Indonesia is unique in many ways. It is an archipelago of more than 17,500 islands. Stretching 3,200 miles (5,150 kilometers), it spans about the same distance as from New York to Los Angeles! It's capital, Jakarta, is on Java, one of the five largest islands in the chain. The other large islands are Sumatra, Kalimantan (the Indonesian part of Borneo), New Guinea, and Sulawesi. The largest flower in the world, called the *Rafflesia arnoldii*, grows only on Sumatra and Borneo. The Komodo dragon's native home is a group of Indonesia's smaller islands.

Indonesia lies on both sides of the equator, which makes it warm all year. Its rainy season extends from October to April. The country's most abundant crops—rice and peanuts—are used in many Indonesian recipes. Indonesians include rice at every meal, but the diversity of ways to prepare this simple dish will amaze you! Little meat is eaten in Indonesia; people in Indonesia are mostly vegetarian. When meat is eaten, it is served as a side dish, with rice as the main entree.

The people of Indonesia are friendly and proud of their traditions, which include artistry in several areas. Weaving, creating batik, playing musical instruments, and performing shadow puppet performances are all features of this country.

All of the materials and ingredients used in this book can be purchased at major supermarkets, discount chain stores, or farmer's markets. We hope

The Indonesian archipelago stretches from Irian Jaya on the western half of New Guinea to the tip of Sumatra, west of Thailand. Although it could span the continental United States, it is only about three times the size of Texas.

you enjoy creating these wonderful recipes and crafts that reflect the heart of Indonesia!

Indonesian Recipes

These easy-to-follow recipes range from basic food for everyday living to dishes served at festivals and celebrations. We include bits of information about the cultural setting in which you might find each dish and explanations of ingredients and techniques. Keep in mind that Indonesian people like spicy food. It's better to go easy on the red pepper until you've acquired a taste for it.

FUN FACT

It's easy to substitute healthy brown rice for white in any recipe. Cook 1 part brown rice in 3 parts water. Increase cooking time to approximately 45 minutes.

When cooking Indonesian dishes, you'll need to observe the same rules in the kitchen as when preparing other types of food.

- Work under the supervision of **an adult** from start to finish.
- Read each recipe carefully and note what ingredients and special utensils are needed. Some ingredients may be easier to find and cheaper to purchase in health food stores, food co-ops, or farmer's markets than in big-chain grocery stores.
- Tie hair back or wear a head cover.
- Remove jewelry, especially from hands and arms. Roll up long sleeves. Avoid loose clothing.
- Wash hands thoroughly each time you prepare food—before and after.
- Wash raw fruits and vegetables before preparation.
- When slicing vegetables, use knives that are sharp and comfortable in your hand. A dull knife or one that is too big for your hand might slip, causing accidents.
- Use a cutting board to slice vegetables.
- Wooden spoons do not conduct heat and are good choices for stirring stovetop dishes.
- Many of the recipes in this book are stir-fried, using oil for heat. If oil in a skillet should smoke or seem too hot, quickly turn off the heat. Do not move the pan or throw water in it. Allow it to cool down and begin again. Keep an open box of baking soda handy to throw on a stove fire.
- Wear oven mitts when lifting lids from hot pans, such as pans of rice. Steam from inside the pan can burn your skin.
- If you do get burned from steam or hot oil, hold the burned area of skin under cold running water. Do not apply butter. Cold water takes the pain out of a burn; grease holds it in.
- Clean up promptly after creating each recipe.
- When finished cooking, check that stovetop dials are OFF before leaving the kitchen.

Spicy Peanut Sauce (Katjang Saos)

Sauces, especially spicy ones, are an important part of Indonesian cuisine. The Spanish are credited for bringing chilies to Indonesia in the 1500s. These ingredients and other hot spices, such as pepper flakes, are added to nearly every dish, including this peanut sauce. Since these tastes are frequently too hot for the American palate, the recipe can be modified to taste.

Spicy food is served at a special event in Indonesia called *selamatan*. The word means "blessing or celebration of achievement." *Selamatan* originated as a religious occasion. Today families hold a *selamatan* for many of life's landmarks. The announcement of a baby, birthdays, the completion of a new house, a successful rice harvest, and weddings all warrant a *selamatan*.

During a *selamatan*, there is prayer, the reading of a portion of the Koran (the Muslim book of faith), and, of course, the sharing of food.

The food at a *selamatan* may be lavish or simple. Peanut sauce is a popular condiment to add to the menu at a *selamatan*. For a recipe that uses it as a condiment, see page 26.

FUN FACT

Although they will use eating utensils, Indonesians prefer to eat with their hands. Food is always eaten with the right hand. The left hand is considered unclean and is not to be used for eating.

Preparation time: 10 minutes
Makes 3-4 servings

Ingredients

½   cup smooth peanut butter
½   cup coconut cream, canned
3   tablespoons soy sauce
       Red pepper flakes (add only 1 or 2 at first to see if you like
       the taste; have a glass of milk handy to diffuse the heat on
       your tongue)

Directions

1. Using blender, combine peanut butter, coconut cream, red
   pepper, and soy sauce until mixed.
2. Refrigerate until ready to serve. Peanut sauce can be served
   warm and is good over rice, mixed vegetables, or meat.

Coconut Rice
(Nasi Gurih)

The staple foods of most people in Indonesia are rice and fish. Fish comes in a huge variety and is cooked in a vast number of ways. Rice is usually boiled or steamed. Yet the people of Indonesia do not find rice monotonous. Rice is served at every meal, including breakfast.

The rice Indonesians prefer is pure white, its outer husk removed. Even though the husk contains most of the nutrients, Indonesians believe brown rice is only for children and sick people. Healthy people who eat brown rice lose their self-respect.

FUN FACT

Indonesian cooks experiment with rice, using it to accompany fish, meat, vegetables, and eggs, or it is baked into desserts.

Preparation time: 15 minutes
Makes 2-4 servings

Ingredients
½ cup long-grain rice
1 cup coconut milk (available in most supermarkets)
4 tablespoons grated dried coconut

Directions
1. Put rice in saucepan with coconut milk.
2. Bring to boil. Simmer 10 minutes or until most of the coconut milk is absorbed.
3. Stir in grated coconut. Heat through, one to two minutes.

Yellow Rice
(Nasi Kuning)

Rice is a valuable crop for the Indonesian people. First, it almost always provides a bountiful harvest, being more productive than any other grain. It grows so quickly farmers can usually make two harvests per year.

Rice is also good for the country of Indonesia as it brings people together. A landscape of flooded rice fields on hilly slopes demands knowledge, experience, and many helpers to maintain. At planting time, each family performs the necessary chores; but during harvest, time is critical and families must call on neighbors and friends to help.

In this recipe, *nasi kuning* (NAH-see KOO-nun), the chicken broth turns the rice yellow.

Preparation time: 35 minutes for white rice; 1 hour for brown rice
Makes 4 servings

Ingredients
1½ cups uncooked white long grain rice, washed and drained
(may substitute ½ cup brown rice)
2½ cups coconut milk
¾ cups chicken stock
1 teaspoon lemon zest moistened with
1 teaspoon water
2 eggs
satay meat (see recipe on page 27)

Directions
1. Combine first four ingredients in saucepan over high heat until it comes to a boil.
2. Lower heat and continue stirring so that the milk does not scorch. Simmer about 10 minutes until liquid is absorbed and rice is fully cooked (increase cooking time for brown rice to 40 minutes).

3. Meanwhile, in another saucepan, place both eggs and cover with water. Bring water to a boil and let cook for 10 minutes. Drain and immediately cover with cold water for 20 minutes.
4. Form the hot rice into a ball and place it on a platter, surrounded by chopped hard-boiled eggs and satay meat.

Note: If a hard-boiled egg is not chilled immediately after cooking, an unsightly dark green ring will appear on the outside of the yolk. Placing the egg in icy cold water prevents the ring from forming.

Fried Rice
(Nasi Goreng)

Nasi goreng (NAH-see GOR-en) is one of the best-known and most popular Indonesian dishes. Like many Indonesian dishes, it originated in another country—China.

During the first century CE, Indonesia was part of the trading route between India and China. The Chinese contributed much to Indonesia's culture by trading soybeans, rice, noodles, and tea for the smaller country's gold and spices. In addition, China gave Indonesia the wok and the process of stir-frying. Without stir-fry, there would be no *nasi goreng* (fried rice). Indonesia just wouldn't be the same.

Nasi goreng is often served with cold meat or stir-fried vegetables.

Preparation time: 35 minutes
Makes 4 servings

Ingredients
2   eggs
⅓ cup oil
3   teaspoons minced garlic
1   onion, finely chopped
2   red chilies, seeded and finely chopped (omit for milder taste)
1   teaspoon coriander seeds, also known as cilantro
½ teaspoon sugar
6   ounces fully cooked shrimp, tails cut off (you can substitute cooked chicken or steak cut into small pieces)
3   cups cold cooked rice
1   tablespoon soy sauce
4   green onions, finely chopped
    Lettuce, finely shredded
1   cucumber, sliced and halved
3   tablespoons fried onions

Directions

1. In a small bowl, beat eggs until foamy.
2. Heat large skillet over medium heat and lightly brush with 1 tablespoon oil. Pour about a quarter of the egg mixture into the pan and cook 1-2 minutes until omelet sets. Flip and cook for 30 seconds. Remove from pan with spatula and repeat with remaining egg mix.
3. When omelets are cold, gently roll them up and shred them into fine strips; set aside.
4. In a food processor, combine garlic, onion, chilies, coriander, and sugar; process until a paste forms.
5. Heat skillet over high heat, add 1 tablespoon of oil, and fry the paste for 1 minute. Add shrimp and stir-fry until lightly browned.
6. Increase heat; add remaining oil and cold rice. Stir-fry, breaking up lumps until rice is heated through.
7. Add soy sauce and green onions; stir-fry another minute.
8. Arrange lettuce around the outside of large platter. Place rice in center; garnish with omelet strips, cucumber, and crisp fried onions.

FUN FACT

Surrounded by rivers and oceans, Indonesians eat an abundance of seafood, including eel, lobster, and shrimp.

Fried Noodles (Mee Goreng)

Dishes such as *mee goreng* (MEE GOR-en) and *nasi* (nah-SEE) *goreng* are staple fare in Indonesia, much like a cheeseburger would be in the United States. These popular Indonesian dishes are created and sold at *warungs*, food stalls that serve as ready-made kitchens. Owners of the *warungs* carry the cooking utensils and brazier on their backs. Each day they roam the streets, hoping to entice customers with the delicious smells of their cooking.

FUN FACT

The hottest part of a red Indonesian chili is the seeds. When preparing hot chilies, wear latex gloves so that you don't get the oil from the seeds on your skin.

Preparation time: 1 hour
Makes 4 Servings

Ingredients
1   large onion, finely chopped
2   teaspoons minced garlic
2   red chilies, seeded and finely chopped (omit for milder taste)
    Fresh ginger grated
¼   cup oil
11 ounces cooked Hokkien noodles, gently pulled apart (Hokkien noodles are thick and yellow. If not available, egg noodles, cooked and well drained, may be used.)
1   pound fully cooked shrimp (you may substitute 8 ounces finely sliced cooked beef or chicken)
4   green onions, chopped
1   large carrot, sliced thinly
2   celery sticks, sliced thinly
1   tablespoon soy sauce
1   tablespoon tomato sauce

Directions
1. Combine chopped onion, garlic, chilies, and ginger in food processor. Process in short bursts until paste forms, adding oil to help grinding if necessary. Set aside.
2. Heat 1 tablespoon oil in skillet; stir-fry noodles until plump and warmed through. Place on serving plate; cover to keep warm.
3. Add 1 tablespoon oil and stir-fry paste mixture until golden. Add shrimp and vegetables; stir-fry 2-3 minutes. Add soy and tomato sauces.
4. Carefully spoon meat and vegetable mix over noodles and serve immediately.

Chicken in Soy Sauce
(Ayam Kecap)

The average kitchen in Indonesia is equipped with large and small mortars and pestles (heavy grinding stones for roots and spices), colanders, sieves, sharp knives, and a hefty chopping block. In the United States, these tools are sold in Asian markets and kitchen specialty stores.

The mortar is a bowl, typically made of hard wood, marble, clay, or stone. The pestle is a heavy bat-shaped stick with an end used for pounding and grinding. The mortar and pestle are used to crush, grind, and mix substances, such as spice mixtures. Grinding the spices before cooking releases their oils and strengthens their flavor.

Finely pounding wet spices is very important when preparing them for Asian cooking. This process may seem like a lot of work to Americans, but Asian cooks are often in less of a hurry to produce a meal, and find the preparation satisfying and pleasurable.

For this recipe, make the sweet soy sauce first, then prepare the marinade, and finally the chicken.

Preparation time: Marinate 4 hours or longer
Cooking time: 45 minutes
Makes 6 servings

Ingredients

1½	cups sugar	2	teaspoons garlic, minced
¾	cup water	1	tablespoon chili sauce
¾	cup soy sauce	2	tablespoons cooking oil
1	large onion, finely chopped	⅓	cup lemon juice
		1	3-pound chicken, cut up

Directions

1. In skillet, heat sugar over medium heat without stirring. Once sugar begins to melt, cook and stir for 2-3 minutes or until golden. Remove from heat. Slowly stir in water and soy sauce. Remove from heat. This is sweet soy sauce.
2. Cook onion, garlic, and chili sauce in hot oil in medium skillet until onion is tender but not brown. Remove from heat. Stir in lemon juice and sweet soy sauce.
3. Return skillet to heat. Watch for spattering of hot oil. Bring the mixture to a boil, then reduce heat and simmer, stirring constantly, about 15 minutes or until mixture is slightly thick and sugar is dissolved. Cool to room temperature. Cover and store in refrigerator. Makes 1⅓ cups.
4. Rinse chicken and pat dry. Place chicken in a plastic bag and set the bag in a deep bowl. Pour marinade over chicken.
5. Close bag tightly and turn to coat chicken. Marinate in refrigerator four hours or overnight, turning bag occasionally.
6. Preheat oven to 375°F. Line bottom of broiler pan with foil. Top with lightly greased broiler rack. Remove chicken from bag and place on unheated rack.
7. Return the marinade to a pan. Bring it to a boil. Remove from heat.
8. Place chicken in oven and roast for 45 minutes or until tender, turning and brushing with the boiled marinade.

Cooked Vegetable Salad (Gado-Gado)

A popular quick lunch dish in Indonesia is *gado-gado*. At *warungs* (street food vendors), you can perch on a stool and watch the vendor as he or she makes the portion as directed before drizzling it with peanut sauce as dressing.

Gado-gado serves as a healthy vegetable dish that can be presented as an artistic platter. Fresh meat and fish are too expensive to eat daily, but soybeans are cheap, and tofu is part of almost every *gado-gado*. The choice of vegetables that can be used to make *gado-gado* is wide. Almost any vegetables left over from the day before or bought during the daily trip to the market can be included.

Preparation time:
45 minutes
Makes 6 servings

Ingredients

1   tablespoon vegetable oil
1   cup tofu, cubed
2   tomatoes
1   cucumber, peeled
3   cooked potatoes, boiled, cooled, and peeled
2   hard-boiled eggs, peeled (see the tip on page 13 for how to
    make perfect hard-boiled eggs)
1   cup fresh shredded cabbage, blanched
½ cup sliced fresh carrots, blanched, or frozen and thawed
½ cup fresh green beans, blanched, or frozen and thawed
Katjang saos (spicy peanut sauce)—see recipe on page 8

Directions

1. Heat oil in skillet on stove over medium high heat. Line a
   plate with paper towels.
2. Add tofu and fry for 8 minutes, until lightly browned. Carefully
   remove with spoon and drain on the plate with paper towels.
3. Thinly slice tomatoes, cucumber, potatoes, and eggs.
4. Arrange tofu cubes, cabbage, carrots, green beans, tomatoes,
   cucumber, and potatoes in salad bowl. Add eggs for garnish.
5. Drizzle with *katjang saos* (peanut sauce) and serve.

To blanch fruit or vegetables, place them in boiling water to
soften (two minutes for sliced carrots and green beans; a
few minutes longer for larger vegetables). When they start to
soften and their color brightens, use a slotted spoon to
remove them from the boiling water and plunge them into
ice water. This will stop the cooking action. When cool,
remove them from the ice water and set aside for further
cooking.

Pepper Salad with Sesame Seeds (Timor Achar)

Most of Indonesia's 200 million people get up at sunrise, the coolest part of the day. For breakfast they may eat leftovers from the day before—shallots, bowls of rice, and soy cubes, or tofu.

Since meat is scarce in Indonesia, meals revolve around fresh fruits and vegetables and huge bowls of cooked dry white rice. In the mornings, cooks in each home usually prepare large pots of plain rice and 3 or 4 dishes for the family to eat during the day. These are left on the table for whenever someone is hungry. The cook is then free for the rest of the day. Food is not reheated; it is eaten at room temperature. Indonesian cooking methods help to keep the food edible.

Preparation time: 1 hour
Makes 6 servings

Ingredients
1   teaspoon sugar
¼ cup apple cider vinegar
2   tablespoons sesame seeds
¼ pound snow peas
1   green bell pepper
1   red bell pepper
1   red onion
1   tomato

Directions
1. Put vinegar and sugar in a jar. Cover and shake to blend; refrigerate.
2. Heat sesame seeds in a skillet over medium heat, tossing until browned, about 3 minutes. Set aside.
3. Core and seed peppers. Cut peas lengthwise into thin strips.
4. Finely slice peppers and onion. Cut tomato into 6 wedges. Put vegetables into a salad bowl. Add dressing. With a large spoon, toss to blend.
5. Sprinkle with sesame seeds. Serve chilled with rice and other dishes.

Indonesian Rice Rolls (Lontong)

Lontong is rice that has been compressed into a solid mass and cooked in a banana leaf packet. The dish is always eaten cold and must be made with rice that is cold. *Lontong* is a traditional bread dish that might be served at an Indonesian buffet. It soaks up the sauce on a dish, and its coolness contrasts with the hot spices in any recipe. In Indonesia, *lontong* is cooked in a cylinder made from a banana leaf or a little packet woven from coconut fronds called *ketupat*. You can make it using aluminum foil instead.

Lontong is associated with festivities that take place at the end of Ramadan, a Muslim religious observance during which followers fast each day from sunrise to sunset. Ramadan ends with a three-day festival called *Eid ul-Fitr*, which means "the feast of the breaking of the fast."

Preparation time: 3 hours
Makes 6 servings

Ingredients

3   cups water
1   cup uncooked long grain white rice, rinsed in cold water (or
    substitute 1 cup brown rice + 3 cups water; increase
    cooking time to 45 minutes)
2½ quarts water

Directions

1. Put white rice and water in a medium saucepan and bring to
   a boil over high heat. Reduce to simmer, cover, and cook for
   15 minutes. Remove from heat, keep covered, and set aside
   for 10 minutes. Uncover and cool at room temperature for 15
   minutes.
2. Place 2 sheets of foil side by side on a work surface and
   divide the cooked rice equally between them. Moisten hands
   and, down the center of the foil, form each mound of rice
   into a sausage shape about 2 inches thick and 6 inches long.
   To wrap rice, bring the two long edges of the foil up over the
   rice and hold them together. Fold them over several times
   and press each fold to tightly seal in rice. Twist ends and
   bend them over, making the package waterproof.
3. Fill a large saucepan with 2½ quarts water. Bring to boil over
   high heat and add foil-wrapped rice. Bring back to boil,
   reduce to simmer, cover, and cook for 1 hour. Wearing oven
   mitts and using tongs, remove packages of rice from water
   and place them on a work surface to cool to room
   temperature. Refrigerate wrapped until ready to serve.
4. To serve, carefully unwrap and discard foil. Place *lontong* on
   a serving dish and cut into 1-inch slices (wetting the knife will
   help with cutting). Serve at room temperature.

Meat Satay
(Sate Ajam)

Sate ajam (sa-TAY ah-YAM)—strips of chicken or shrimp threaded on a bamboo skewer and grilled—is a popular dish in Indonesia. Not only is it delicious, it is easy to eat while on the go.

Throughout each day, street vendors carry portable braziers on their backs. Whenever they see a customer who appears hungry, they will stop and hurriedly set up the temporary kitchen, hoping the smell of grilled meat will encourage a sale.

At home, cooks can easily fix satay for large groups and serve it with *lontong*, vegetables, and salads. Satay is also served during special occasions, such as weddings and temple festivals. During temple festivals, satay sellers line the path taken by crowds climbing the hill to worship. Among the numerous food stalls along the avenue, those selling satay are always the biggest attraction.

FUN FACT

Street vendors in Indonesia sell barbecued lamb or chicken on skewers dipped in sauces made from coconut milk, peanuts, or soybeans.

Preparation time: 2 hours
Makes 4 servings

Ingredients

1 pound skinless, boneless chicken
   breast cut into thin strips
1 teaspoon curry powder (omit for
   milder taste)
½ cup coconut cream, canned
½ cup apple cider vinegar
2 tablespoons sugar
2 tablespoons dried crushed red
   pepper (This can be very hot!
   Reduce or omit for milder taste)
1 onion, finely chopped
¼ teaspoon coriander
   green and red peppers, cherry
   tomatoes, and pineapple, chopped

Metal skewers are preferred, but if you use wooden skewers, soak them first in cold water for at least half an hour.

Directions

1. Put strips of meat in shallow dish.
2. Mix curry powder, coconut milk, vinegar, sugar, red pepper, onion, and coriander in a bowl. Pour over strips and mix well to coat. Refrigerate one hour, mixing frequently to coat strips.
3. Set oven rack approximately 6 inches under broiler and preheat to high.
4. Thread chicken onto skewers lengthwise, one piece per skewer. Fill skewers with chopped vegetables and fruit.
5. Place skewers side by side on a baking sheet and broil for 3 minutes until lightly browned. Turn strips over and broil the other side until cooked through and browned, about 3 minutes.
6. Serve satay with peanut dipping sauce (recipe on page 8).

- Read through the instructions—all the way—before you start. This tip can be hard to follow, because you might be so eager to start, you'll dive right in. That's the right spirit! But read all the way through anyway. You'll be glad you did.
- Gather all your materials first. A missing ingredient might make you stop halfway through, and then you won't feel like finishing. Seeing a half-finished project lying around stinks.
- Protect your work surface. Lay down newspaper or a plastic tablecloth. (This is a step your parents will be glad you took!) Wear play clothes.
- Be creative. You might think of a great new step to add or a twist that gives the craft your personal touch. While you're at it, learn from your mistakes. Try a craft a few times to get it right. Your craft doesn't have to look like the one in the picture to be great.
- Be careful. When the instructions tell you to get help from **an adult**, then please, get help from **an adult**!
- Clean up right away. This step is boring, but it's much easier to clean paintbrushes, wipe down surfaces, and wash tools (including your hands) while the mess is fresh. Plus, when you ask for permission to start a new project, you can remind your parents that you cleaned up last time. (Add a "pretty please" if you think it will help.) You could also ask your parents to join you. Crafts are even more fun when someone does them with you.
- As you go about your everyday activities, save things that might be good for your projects. Shoeboxes, toilet paper rolls, ribbon and tissue paper from a gift—these can all be used to make crafts that you'll enjoy keeping or giving to friends and family.
- The final secret? Have fun! If you don't enjoy it, there's no point in crafting.

Woven Paper Placemat

Indonesia has some of the most exotic weavers in the world. They excel in two areas: weaving techniques and variety of details.

The country's trade between China, India, and Europe brought many new thread types, including silk, to the craft. The primary thread had been made of cotton. The results were beautiful woven pieces that gleamed with gold and silver highlights.

Color is another important detail in a weaving. In some Indonesian tribes, the use of colors and woven patterns is based on the social status of the wearer in that society. For example, yellow and gold in Malay society can only be worn by members of the royal family.

Perhaps you would like to make a paper weaving that reflects Indonesia's flag. The flag consists of two equal horizontal bars—red on the top and white on the bottom. The red represents bravery and strength. White represents peace and honesty.

- 2 pieces construction paper in contrasting colors
- Scissors
- Ruler
- Laminating machine or clear shelf paper

Directions
1. Measure 1 piece of paper in 1-inch increments. Cut into strips.
2. With other paper draw 1-inch lines on long sides. Cut 1 inch from ends.
3. Weave strips over and under cut edges. Place strips close together.
4. When paper is filled, laminate, cutting 1-inch borders on sides. Or cut two 11-inch x 14-inch pieces of clear shelf paper and sandwich weaving between, leaving 1-inch borders on sides.
5. Use the weaving as a placemat and think of Indonesia each time you sit down to eat!

The Indonesian Flag

Yarn Weaving

One type of weaving done in Indonesia is *ikat* (EE-kaht), which means "tie." *Ikat* is the process of dyeing threads before they are woven into a patterned cloth. *Ikat* cloth is an essential part of the traditional costume worn in Bali, an Indonesian island south of Java. Many centuries ago, traders brought the *ikat* technique from Holland to Indonesia. It has since developed into a complex and popular art form in Bali.

Ikat is an advanced form of weaving, but you can weave a simple scarf or belt with just one piece of yarn. If you use variegated (multicolored) yarn, your piece will automatically have patterns in it.

Some adult supervision required

You'll Need:

- Ball of yarn—variegated colors work well
- Scissors
- Needle-nosed pliers
- 2 drinking straws, cut in half, or 4 whole straws (do not use bendy straws)
- Thin wire slightly longer than straws
- Tape

Directions

1. Cut four pieces of yarn 36 inches long.
2. Use pliers to curl a tiny hook at end of wire.
3. Hook a strand from the cut yarn over wire; pull through a straw so that 1 inch of yarn hangs over the end of the

straw. Tape this end to straw. Repeat with separate strands and straws. Knot the ends of the strands together.

4. With your left hand, hold straws like a fan, taped ends out. (Hint: If you write with your left hand, it may be easier to hold the straws in your right hand).

5. With the opposite hand, place the rest of the ball of yarn under the the hand holding the straws (see picture).

6. Wind yarn above and below straws, working from one side to the other.

7. Work in this way until you have woven several inches. Occasionally check your work to be sure you are using consistent pressure as you weave. (Avoid pulling yarn too tight, as this will create an hourglass effect in your weaving.)

8. Push the woven yarn off the bottom of the straws.

9. Continue weaving and pushing the finished part off the straws until your project reaches the desired length. A bookmark should be 6 inches; a necktie or scarf should be long enough for the ends to overlap; and a belt should be the circumference of your waist with an additional 12 inches.

10. Cut the yarn from the ball. Tie the end to the end piece of yarn.

11. Knot all the strands together at the top.

Indonesian Rain Stick

Indonesia contains the most extensive rain forest in all of Asia. It is the world's largest exporter of tropical timber, which brings more than $5 billion into the country each year. However, because of illegal logging, mining operations, and other activities, Indonesia's forests have become some of the most threatened on the planet.

In the 1960s, 82 percent of the country of Indonesia was covered with forest. By 2010, that number had dropped to 49 percent. The effects from forest loss are widespread. Without the trees to hold the ground, rain can wash away nutrient-rich topsoil; sometimes, it causes mudslides.

Though Indonesia's forests face a discouragingly grim future, the country has 400 protected areas. With its wildlife, forests, coral reefs, cultural attractions, and warm seas, Indonesia has the potential to see even more protection granted to its natural environment.

Rain is important for the health of a rain forest, and Indonesia receives up to 11 inches of rainfall per month. You can make a rain stick to mimic the sound of rain falling through the leaves.

Some adult supervision required

- Paper towel or gift-wrap cardboard tube
- 2 pieces of plastic wrap, each 6 inches square
- Masking tape
- Markers or paints
- 1/2 cup dry uncooked rice (white or brown)

Directions

1. Cover one end of tube with plastic wrap. Secure with masking tape. Check that end is completely covered.
2. Using paint or markers (if using paint, protect your work surface), create wild designs on the tube. Allow to dry.
3. Pour rice inside tube.
4. Cover other end of tube as you did in step 1.

Gently tilt stick and listen to the "rain" in an Indonesian rain forest.

Shadow Puppet

Entire villages in Indonesia gather to watch shadow puppet shows called *wayang* (wah-YAHNG). They usually tell stories from religious mythology blended with historical facts. The show may last all night.

The puppeteer, or *dalang*, tells the story accompanied by a *gamelan* (GAM-uh-lahn) orchestra and occasional chanting or singing. The *dalang* commands high respect from his community, for he performs the job of an actor, teacher, historian, and often priest.

Indonesian shadow puppets are usually cut from thin, stiff leather. The size of a puppet depends on whether it represents a god (small) or demon (enormous and grotesque). King Ramayana is a popular shadow puppet figure. In his homeland of India, Ramayana has been known for 3,000 years. With the spread of Indian religions and culture throughout Southeastern Asia, Ramayana became part of the mythology of Burma, Thailand, Laos, Cambodia, Java, and Bali. Ramayana revolves around the character of Rama, a king's son who must be victorious in many battles before earning his father's throne. He would be a large puppet.

You'll Need:

- Pencil
- White poster board
- Crayons or markers
- Scissors
- Hole punch
- 4 brads

- 4 straws
- Clear tape
- White cloth
- Large box
- Small lamp

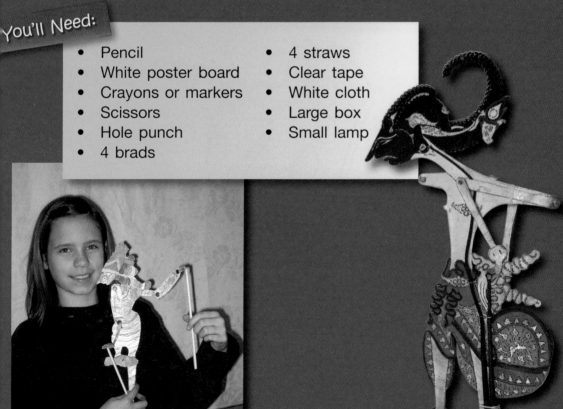

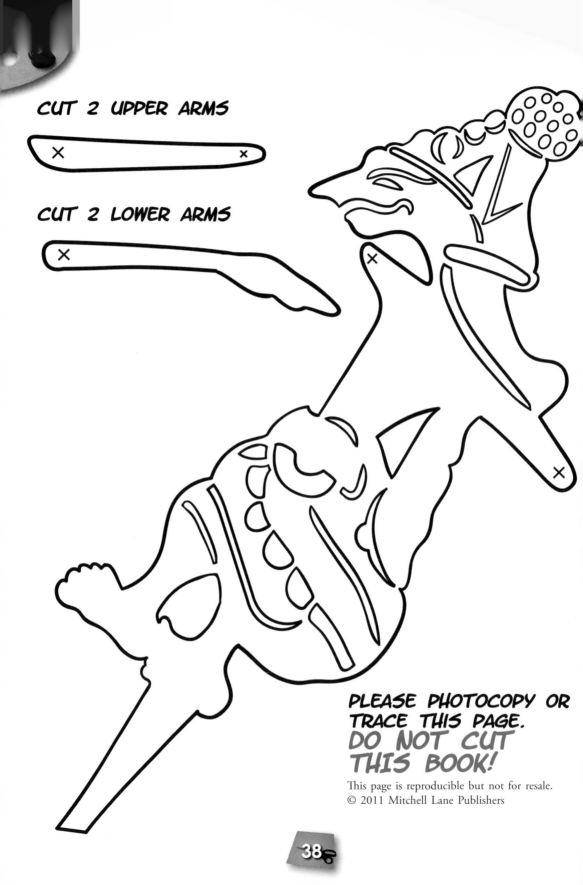

CUT 2 UPPER ARMS

CUT 2 LOWER ARMS

PLEASE PHOTOCOPY OR
TRACE THIS PAGE.
DO NOT CUT
THIS BOOK!

This page is reproducible but not for resale.
© 2011 Mitchell Lane Publishers

38

Adult supervision recommended

Directions

1. Trace and cut out the pattern of King Ramayana figure on poster board, including arm sections (see page 38).
2. Decorate with crayons or markers.
3. Use a hole punch to make holes in the shoulders and elbows of both arms (marked with an x).
4. Apply brads to the joints of elbows and shoulders.
5. Tape two straws to the puppet's back for support. Tape additional straws to the puppet's hands (see photo).
6. Pin a white sheet above a doorway. Kneel behind an empty box in the middle of the doorway. Position a bright light behind you. Turn off all the lights, except the one behind you, and share a shadow puppet story with family and friends!

Kenong Musical Instrument

The music of Indonesia is complex, noisy, and vibrant. The traditional Indonesian orchestra, known as *gamelan*, entertains whole villages at a time, usually at night. A *gamelan* is composed of various percussion instruments, such as gongs and xylophones, plus string and woodwind instruments like violins and flutes. A *gamelan* orchestra may have just a few players or up to several dozen. The *gamelan* does not focus on the musical talent of its members. Rather, music produced by a *gamelan* orchestra requires a strong sense of rhythm and attention to the music produced by the entire group.

Adult supervision recommended

You'll Need:

- 14-ounce cereal box, empty
- Clear tape
- Ruler
- Markers
- 5 empty, clean, dry tin cans, with label and one end removed
- Razor knife or pointed scissors
- Newspaper
- Spray paint, primer (black works well)
- Duct tape in various colors
- Glue
- Crochet needles, pencils, or knitting needles

Directions

1. Fold the flaps of the box shut and tape them closed. On the front, draw 1-inch lines from each edge to form a rectangle. **Under adult supervision**, use a razor knife or sharp scissors to cut out the rectangle.
2. Cover your work area with newspaper, then paint the five cans and the box. Let the paint dry. (Hint: Set the painted items in front of a blow dryer to speed the process.)
3. Place cans bottom side up inside the box. Use duct tape to decorate the box and the parts of cans that show above the box. Additional designs may be created on duct tape with permanent markers.
4. Experiment with household utensils to find good beaters for your *kenong*. Listen to how the cans produce different tones. Hold different types of beaters in each hand for interesting combinations. Invite a friend to create his or her own *kenong* and form your own orchestra!

Bali *Gamelan* Music Drum

The *gamelan* orchestra is essential to *wayang* performances. It takes some listeners time to adjust to *gamelan* music because it can be very loud and repetitive. Some people compare the sound of the *gamelan* to "liquid moonlight."

After you've made a *kenong*, you could make this drum to go with it.

- Large oatmeal box with lid
- 2 bright sheets of construction paper, same color
- Tape
- Glue
- Markers
- 4 six-inch wooden rulers
- 12-inch wooden ruler
- Newspaper
- Black paint
- Paintbrush
- Yarn (variegated works well)
- Brads

Some adult supervision required

Directions

1. Tape or glue construction paper around a large oatmeal box.
2. Tape one end of the yarn to the bottom of the box. Pull the yarn taut to other end of box and secure it with a brad. Continue with yarn and brads in this way around the box, making a zigzag pattern (see photograph). When you've gone all the way around, cut the yarn and tape it to other end.

3. Spread newspaper over your work surface. Paint the six-inch wooden rulers. Let the paint dry.
4. Cross two rulers, flat sides together, and put a dab of glue between them. Wind yarn around the pieces several times, crisscrossing to hold them together. Glue the end of the yarn to one side. Repeat with the other two rulers.
5. **Ask an adult** to use a small handsaw to cut notches 1 inch from the ends of the 12-inch ruler. The notches should be on the same side of the ruler and narrow enough to fit over the yarn on the crossed pieces. Place the ruler over the crossed pieces.
6. Place the drum on the stand and pretend you are part of a *gamelan* orchestra.

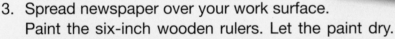

The Smell of Death
Coffee Filter Flower

Thousands of plants cover the Indonesian islands. The rare *Rafflesia arnoldii*, the world's biggest flower, can grow to be 3 feet across and weigh up to 15 pounds. It is a parasitic plant with no visible leaves, roots, or stem. It attaches itself to a host plant to obtain water and nutrients. When in bloom, the *Rafflesia* emits a repulsive odor, similar to that of rotting meat. This odor attracts the insects that pollinate the plant.

You can make a replica of these rain-forest flowers using coffee filters and chenille stems. Your flower may not be as large as the *Rafflesia arnoldii*, but it also won't be as stinky!

Some adult supervision required

You'll Need:

- 4 white coffee filters any size
- 1 chenille stem, cut in half
- 2 small bowls
- 3/4 cup water
- Food coloring
- Plate, waxed paper, or plastic surface

Directions

1. Lay the coffee filters on top of each other and flatten them.
2. Fold the filters accordion-style into 1-inch pleats.
3. Twist a chenille stem around the middle of the pleats.
4. Add 6-10 drops of food coloring to 1/2 cup water in a bowl. Stir.
5. With filters still folded, dip edges into the food coloring for several seconds until they are saturated with dye. Lay the filters on a plate, waxed paper, or plastic surface to dry.

Rafflesia arnoldii

6. Mix 1/4 cup water in a bowl with 6-10 drops of food coloring. Dunk the pleated center into the mixture, allowing it to saturate the filters until colors meet. Let the filters dry.

7. Separate the layers on both sides of the chenille stem. Arrange them so that they look like flower petals.

8. Use dark-colored markers to create dots on your flower so that it resembles the *Rafflesia arnoldii*.

Ogoh-Ogoh Mask

Each spring the island of Bali celebrates the *Nyepi* festival, in which a monster-like figure called Ogoh-Ogoh is carried throughout the countryside. According to Balinese culture, Ogoh-Ogoh is a giant who likes to eat humans. He has googly eyes and torn clothes. Ogoh-Ogoh is also thought to symbolize the devil, and he influences humans to misbehave. By carrying him throughout the countryside, villagers believe the monster's power is taken away.

Adult supervision required
This project is much easier to do with the help of a friend.

You'll Need:

- Aluminum foil
- 2 or more rolls of masking tape, 1 inch wide
- Scissors
- Acrylic paint
- Plastic molding as used on light bulb packages. (If you don't have plastic packaging, use 2 Ping-Pong balls cut in half. Cut circles in the centers to see through.)
- Stapler
- Yarn or string

Directions

1. Cut a piece of aluminum foil large enough to cover the top and sides of your head. Carefully place the sheet against your face (close your eyes!) and gently press to flatten around your eyes, nose, mouth, and chin. Press all around to create the actual shape of your head. **Ask an adult** to cut a mouth hole for you to breathe through.
2. Ask a friend to take strips of masking tape and gently lay them onto the shaped foil while you are still wearing it. The tape should be applied in smooth layers.

3. Once there is enough tape applied to hold the shape, remove the foil mask from your head. Place it on something firm like your bent knee to help keep its shape. Continue to apply strips of tape. It will look like you are making a mummy! Be sure to apply the strips as smoothly as possible. Add as many layers of tape as needed to ensure the mask is sturdy. Try on the mask occasionally to ensure a good fit. The mask should fit like a helmet, but you don't want to make it too tight.

Hint: A head form for a wig is a helpful prop to use when applying the masking tape.

4. Once the mask resembles the shape of your head, ask an adult to cut eye holes in the appropriate places. These should be big enough for you to see through comfortably.

5. Cut two plastic lightbulb wrappings into round shapes. (You can use anything packaged in round, clear, thin plastic). Paint the INSIDES like eyes, starting with the colored circles in the eyes. The exteriors will remain unpainted and shiny. Then paint the whites of the eyes. (Be creative and make them yellow or even green!) Leave a circle—half an inch in diameter—of clear unpainted plastic at the center for you to see through when wearing the mask.

6. Use masking tape to secure these two "eyes" to your mask. Try not to cover the painted part of the eyes.

7. Now it's time to shape your mask like a monster's face. Using crumbled-up pieces of masking tape, arch the brow, cheeks,

chin, and teeth. Keep the sticky side on the outside of your crinkled shapes so that they will stick. Keep adding and shaping with large and small bits of tape.

8.   When you have the look you want, smooth the exaggerated areas with strips of tape as you did in forming the mask. You may even crinkle tape into pointy ears—just smooth them again with layers of tape and attach to the

sides of your mask. You should now have a mask with interesting features.

9. Once the mask is smooth and wearable, it's time to paint! Go crazy, using red with purple, or green with blue, whatever you want your Ogoh-Ogoh to look like. Apply plenty of paint to smooth out the lines of tape, so it will look like monster skin.

10. Once the paint dries, staple two 12-inch pieces of yarn or string to the mask close to your ears. Then put on your Ogoh-Ogoh mask and march outside!

Sssssssay "Hello" to a
Komodo Dragon

When Komodo dragons were first spotted in 1910 on the coast of Komodo, an island near Indonesia's mainland, some people thought they were the long-lost dinosaurs. In a way they were right. Komodo dragons are the largest-known lizards in the world. They have been known to reach 10 feet from their tooth-filled snout to the tip of their long, pointed tail. Most adults weigh about 150 pounds, but one lazy captive Komodo reached 370 pounds.

This reptile can smell its favorite food—carrion, which is dead meat—from up to six miles away when the wind is blowing just right. It can move as fast as 18 miles per hour to catch live prey. Its jaws open wide, which helps when eating large animals, such as pigs, deer, and even baby Komodos. The venomous Komodo rarely hurts humans. In fact, residents of Komodo National Park in eastern Indonesia where Komodo dragons live believe the dragons are a reincarnation of their kinsfolk and treat them with reverence.

Komodo dragons in the wild number 3,000 to 5,000, and they are considered endangered.

- Cookie sheet
- Wax paper, 12 inches square
- 1 package Sculpey modeling clay
- Books with photos of Komodo dragons

- Acrylic paint
- Paintbrush
- Oven mitt
- Red tissue paper
- School glue

Adult supervision recommended

Directions

1. Prepare your work area by placing a small cookie sheet covered with wax paper in front of you.
2. Break the Sculpey clay into small pieces and roll them between your hands so that they become warm and easy to work with.
3. Divide the clay into parts of the animal's body. The torso should be the biggest ball of clay, with the head the second largest.
4. Study photos of the Komodo dragon to get an idea of the shapes you want. Attach the head to the body, then roll out a long, pointy tail.

5. The legs should be thick enough to hold the body up. Create claws on the dragon's feet, and add other details to its face. If you want, twist the body and tail slightly and adjust the feet so that it appears your dragon is moving and actively seeking its prey.

6. When the body is completely formed, apply a combination of gray, brown, and beige paints to create a camouflage effect. (If you purchased gray Sculpey, you may be able to eliminate the painting step.) Paint the underside first, then the top. Be sure to dab your brush into all crevices.

7. When the paint is dry, remove wax paper from cookie sheet. **Ask an adult** to place cookie sheet and dragon into preheated oven set at 270°F. Bake for 20 minutes.

8. Remove from oven. After it has cooled and dried, you may want to touch up your paint. Then cut a notched edge on one end of a strip of tissue paper. Use school glue to attach the paper to the end of the underside of your dragon's mouth. Then display your Komodo dragon for friends and family!

Batik T-Shirt

The word *batik* (bah-TEEK) is an Indonesian-Malay word that means "to dot." Batik is the method of applying dye to cloth that has been dotted with a design in wax. After dying, the wax is removed and a beautiful effect is achieved. Over the years, batik designs have come to incorporate nature motifs, geometric shapes, and religious and mythological characters. Instead of dotting the wax, it is painted on using a tool called a canting. A good piece of batik may take months to complete, and it often becomes a family heirloom.

Certain patterns made with black and white are considered to have protective powers against evil spirits. They are used to cover statues that guard the entrances to temples.

Adult supervision recommended

You'll Need:

- Covers to protect table and floor, such as painters' drop cloths or old shower curtains
- White cotton T-shirt, washed and dried
- Large piece of cardboard
- Fabric dye in bright color
- Water
- Plastic container big enough to hold shirt (a bucket is a good choice)
- Household paraffin wax
- Empty soup can
- Paintbrush
- Saucepan
- Stove
- Flat household item for stamping, such as an empty thread spool
- Rubber gloves
- Clothesline or drying rack
- Table knife

This project is best done outside. However, if you are working indoors, be sure to cover all surfaces with painters' drop cloths or old shower curtains. Wear old clothes and shoes.

Directions

1. Slide a piece of cardboard between the two layers of a white cotton T-shirt on a protected surface. The front of the shirt should face up.
2. Put 1 inch of water in the bottom of a saucepan. Place paraffin in a soup can, and set it in the saucepan. Heat the pan on a stove over a low setting. You do not need to stir.

3. When the wax is melted, dip a paintbrush in it and apply it to the shirt, creating simple designs such as flowers, the sun, the moon, and stars. You could also stamp a print. It is not necessary to apply several layers of wax to get the desired effect. Allow the wax to harden for a few minutes.
4. Wearing rubber gloves, mix the dye in a plastic bucket according to the manufacturer's instructions.
5. Dip the shirt in the dye, gently swishing the fabric to saturate. The longer the fabric remains in the dye, the deeper the color.
6. Gently squeeze excess liquid from the shirt. Spread the garment to dry on a clothesline or drying rack. Remember to carefully protect your floor from drips. Let the shirt dry. This could take a couple of days.

Tip: When washing your batik shirt for the first time, wash it by itself in hot water and vinegar. This will set the dye so that it won't bleed onto other clothes in future washings.

7. Using a dull knife, such as a table knife, scrape excess wax from shirt. Wear your batik shirt with pride!

BONUS TIP

Once you've mastered batiking, experiment with two colors of dye. Saturate one part of the garment with one color; dry. Cover remaining parts with second color. It should create an interesting effect!

Further Reading

Books

Cornell, Kari A. *Holiday Cooking Around the World*. Minneapolis, MN: Lerner Publications Company, 2002.

Cumming, David. *Indonesia*. North Mankato, MN: Cherrytree Books, 2005.

Doney, Meryl. *Musical Instruments*. Milwaukee, Wisconsin: Gareth Stevens, 2004.

Furgang, Kathy. *Tambora: A Killer from Indonesia*. New York: Rosen Publishing Group, 2001.

Lim, Robin. *A Ticket to Indonesia*. Minneapolis, MN: Carolrhoda Books, Inc., 2001.

Mesenas, Geraldine, and Frederick Fisher. *Welcome to Indonesia!* Milwaukee, WI: Gareth Stevens, 2001.

Works Consulted

"About Gamelan Music."
http://homepages.cae.wisc.edu/~jjordan/gamelan/about.html

Albyn, Carole Lisa, and Lois Sinaiko Webb. *The Multicultural Cookbook for Students*. Phoenix, AZ: Oryx Press, 1993.

Asia/Pacific Cultural Centre for UNESCO (ACCU). "Traditional Weaving Inventory." Kyoto, Osaka, and Nara, Japan. July 15–22, 2009.
http://www.accu.or.jp/ich/en/training/casestudy_pdf/09_10/
case_study_report_indonesia.pdf

Betty Crocker's International Cookbook. New York: Random House Inc., 1980.

"The Classic Hard-Boiled Egg." http://www.goodegg.com/boiledegg.html

Discover Indonesia: Indonesian Art of Textile: Batik.
http://discover-indo.tierranet.com/batikpag.htm

Gerungan, Lonny. *The Bali Cookbook*. Lanham, MD: Kyle Books, 2008.

Hansen, Barbara. *Southeast Asian Cooking*. Tucson, AZ: Fisher Books, 1992.

"Ikat Weaving Tour."
http://www.incitoprima.com/details.php?aid=28

Indonesia: Environmental Profile:
http://rainforests.mongabay.com/20indonesia.htm

"Indonesian Flag."
http://www.flags-flags-flags.org.uk/indonesian-flag.htm

Knox, Gerald M. (editor). *Oriental Recipes*. Des Moines, IA: Meredith Corp, 1987.

Library of Congress: Everyday Mysteries, "*Rafflesia arnoldii*."
http://www.loc.gov/rr/scitech/mysteries/flower.html

McNair, James. *James McNair Cooks Southeast Asian*. San Francisco: Chronicle Books, 1996.

Further Reading

Marks, Copeland. *The Exotic Kitchens of Indonesia*. New York: M. Evans and Company Inc., 1989.

Monaghan, Kathleen, and Hermon Joyner. *You Can Weave! Projects for Young Weavers*. Worcester, MA: Davis Publication Inc., 2000.

Morris, Sallie. *Classic Indonesian Cooking*. London: Southwater, 2007.

"Ogoh-Ogoh / Bali Monster Cortege Greet the Bali New Year," *Bali Star Island*, April 4, 2006. http://www.balistarisland.com/Balinews/BaliNews-Apr0602.htm

Oseland, James. *Cradle of Flavor*. New York: Norton & Company, Inc., 2006.

Owen, Sri. *The Indonesian Kitchen*. Northampton, MA: Interlink Books, 2009.

"Ramayana, A Story About Life."
http://indahnesia.com/indonesia/JAWRAM/ramayana.php

Stephen, Wendy (editor). *New Asian Cooking*. Millers Point, Australia: Bay Books, 2006.

"Textiles of Bali." Bali and Indonesia on the Net.
http://www.indo.com/culture/textile.html

Trofimov, Yaroslav. "When Good Lizards Go Bad: Komodo Dragons Take Violent Turn." *Wall Street Journal*, August 25, 2008. http://online.wsj.com/article/SB121963304805268235.html?mod=djemBestOfTheWeb

Ventura, Carol. "Ikat in Bali, Indonesia."
http://iweb.tntech.edu/cventura/ikat.htm

Von Holzen, Heinz. *The Food of Bali: Authentic Recipes from the Island of the Gods*. Singapore: Periplus Editions, 1996.

Witton, Patrick. *World Food Indonesia*. Lonely Plant Publications Pty Ltd, 2002.

On the Internet

Bali and Indonesia on the Net
http://www.indo.com

Bali Paradise
http://www.bali-paradise.com/bali/index.html

Komodo National Park
http://www.dephut.go.id/INFORMASI/TN%20INDO-ENGLISH/komodo_NP.htm

Republic of Indonesia
http://www.indonesia.go.id/en/

The Ultimate Indonesian Homepage
http://indonesia.elga.net.id/

Glossary

archipelago (ar-kih-PEH-leh-go)—A chain of islands.

baste (BAYST)—To brush with liquid while cooking.

batik (bah-TEEK)—Patterned fabric made by waxing and dyeing cloth.

blanch—Process by which fruit or vegetables are placed in boiling water for two minutes to soften, then plunged into cold water to stop the cooking action.

endangered species (en-dayn-jerd SPEE-sheez)—A type of animal at risk for becoming extinct.

equator (ee-KWAY-tur)—Imaginary line around the center of the Earth.

extinct (ek-STINKT)—No longer living.

fasting—Not eating for certain periods of time, usually for religious reasons.

gamelan (GAM-uh-lahn)—A type of Indonesian orchestra that uses drums, gongs, and other kinds of percussion instruments.

marinade (MAYR-ih-nayd)—A sauce in which meat or other ingredients are soaked for a period of time before they are cooked.

monsoon (mon-SOON)—Heavy rain brought by seasonal winds.

motif (moh-TEEF)—A pattern or design that follows a theme and is usually repeated.

tofu (toh-FOO)—A thick paste or curd made from soybeans.

warung (wah-RUNG)—A street food vendor who carries a brazier on his or her back.

wayang (wy-YAN)—A drama performed using shadow puppets.

Index

PHOTO CREDITS: Cover, p. 1—Ted Ollikkala; pp. 2–3, 8—Jupiter Images; pp. 4–5—Miek Schenk; p. 7—Gerard Adriaanse; pp. 9, 11, 16, 17, 22, 23, 24, 28, 31, 32, 33, 35, 37, 39, 40, 41, 42, 43, 45, 47, 48, 51, 54, 55—Kayleen Reusser; p. 29—Jeno Ortiz; p. 34—Evan Leeson; p. 38—Joe Rasemas; p. 46—Simon Parker; p. 55—Jon Hanson. All other photos—Creative Commons. Every effort has been made to locate all copyright holders of material used in this book. If any errors or omissions have occurred, corrections will be made in future editions of the book.

ABOUT THE
AUTHORS

Kayleen Reusser (left) has written several books for Mitchell Lane Publishers, including biographies of Taylor Swift, Selena Gomez, and Leona Lewis. Although her home is in Bluffton, Indiana, she has traveled to Europe and Central America. She is excited to promote Indonesia, a country her daughter has grown to love.

Amanda Reusser (right) moved from Indiana to Indonesia in 2008. She teaches drama and English to teenagers at a private Christian school, and she produces and directs the school's plays and musicals.

When she's not busy teaching and grading papers at Starbucks, Amanda loves traveling to other countries, especially within Asia. In 2007, she earned a certificate in Thailand to teach English internationally, and she has visited India, Singapore, Hong Kong, and Japan.

Her favorite Indonesian foods are satay ayam and batagor (fried fish pieces). She also enjoys eating Thai sticky rice with mango and drinking mango lassi, an Indian drink.